Marx & Engels confidential

Amazing excerpts from the uncensored original correspondence
of Karl Marx and Friedrich Engels

The true faces of the two world-famous philosophers

Marx & Engels confidential

Amazing excerpts from the uncensored original correspondence
of Karl Marx and Friedrich Engels

The true faces of the two world-famous philosophers

Publisher

Björn Akstinat & Simon Akstinat

Authors

Karl Marx & Friedrich Engels
Björn Akstinat & Simon Akstinat
(Preface and explanatory inserts)

Translation

Frank Steffen & Björn Akstinat

Cover design

Björn Akstinat & Katharina Reinhold

Publishing house

IMH-Verlag
Internationale Medienhilfe (IMH)
P.O. Box 35 05 51
10214 Berlin
www.imh-verlag.de
info@imh-verlag.de

ISBN 978-3-9815158-4-8

Marx & Engels confidential

The following text is from the German bestseller audiobook "Marx & Engels intim" - performed by famous speakers: Harry Rowohlt (writer), Gregor Gysi (Member of the Bundestag for the German Socialist Party) and Anna Thalbach (actress).

Welcome to "Marx & Engels confidential"!

You may look forward in anticipation towards exiting readings from the personal letters and accounts between the most well known philosophers of the world: Karl Marx and Friedrich Engels.

The personal letters of these two men, who have been elevated to an almost god-like status in Eastern Europe and East Asia, are of such substance and relevance, that we are most eager to introduce them to you.

We would have to make clear right from the start, that the letters presented here are likely to have a greater shock-effect today, than they would have had at the time. In those days anti-Semitism was a very common occurrence and could be regarded as much more main stream, than is the case today. Words such as "Nigger", which are frowned upon today, still formed part of the daily vocabulary even as recently as the Eighties of the 20th century, without anybody taking exception to the use of such words. While these letters might sound offensive to some, they simply prove that even world-

renowned people, such as the two in question, are
essentially just humans and not gods.

However, let us start by providing you some of the
essential backgrounds to these persons: Karl Marx was
born in Trier in the year 1818 and died in London
during 1883. Friedrich Engels was born in Wuppertal
in 1820 - two years after Marx - and also died in
London in the year 1895.

These two friends penned their most famous work
"The Communist Manifesto" (German: Das
Kommunistische Manifest) in the year 1848 and
shortly thereafter launched the publication "Neue
Rheinische Zeitung" in Cologne. Within a very short
time this publication was able to increase its print run
to what might be considered abnormally high at the
time. With 6 000 copies printed per run it became one
of the best-known press organs of the revolutionary
period in Germany. The authorities frowned upon this
newspaper and it only took a few months of chicanery
by the Prussian state for the "Neue Rheinische
Zeitung" to be stopped from being printed. Being non-
Prussian, Marx was simply banished. The remaining
members of the editorial team were arraigned and
taken to court.

Marx remained in exile in London until his death in
1883. In this time he authored his famous book
"Capital" (better known under its German title: Das
Kapital). During this time his buddy Engels took part
in the last revolutionary uprisings in Baden (Germany).

Once these last revolts had also been crushed Engels
left too and went into exile.

After Marx's death all of his written papers and
documents were inherited by Engels. When Engels
died this intellectual wealth was in turn inherited by the
German political party SPD. Unfortunately much of
this inheritance was lost on account of neglect and
negligent management, thus causing many records to
be lost.

One of the people, who made it his duty to trace and
collect all of these records and assimilate them into a
complete documentary library, was David Riazanov,
who was employed as Director of the Marx-Engels
Institute in Moscow. David Riazanov simply collected
everything connected to these two Rhenish
philosophers that he could lay his hands on. Part of that
collection are the letters, which we are about to
introduce to you. This caused suspicion among the
Sowjet leadership, so much so, that he was executed
"just in case" in the year 1938. One never knows when
you encounter people who seem to be too inquisitive!

And so it is today our privilege to read letters to you,
some of which were never intended for the public! But
we will not shoot you simply for listening! Promise!

We would like to start by taking a little excursion into
the youth of Karl Marx, before he met Friedrich
Engels, and would like to reflect on the wisdom behind
the advice of: "Beware of the beginnings". In the
process we are being introduced to a principle conflict,

which most Philosophers encounter: The question of money. How do you earn it and how do you ensure sufficiency, when it is so easy spending it?

As dad, Heinrich Marx had his own hands full with son Karl. And so he compiled a sorrowful letter to his son on 18 November 1835:

"Dear Karl! You have been gone for more than three weeks and yet we have received no word of your whereabouts! Even though you know your mother and her permanent anxiety, we have to endure this careless negligence! This behaviour unfortunately confirms my opinion, that while you might have many good attributes, your inherent egotism seems to take up the greater part of your heart."

Two years later, on the 9th December 1837, the anxious father wrote another letter to his apparently unruly fledgling:

"Contrary to all agreements and against all custom, our son - Sir - spends 700 thalers per year as if we were made of gold, while rich people spend 500 at best."

Two months later it would seem as though Karl has finally achieved his goal: His dad blames himself for having raised an ill-mannered son and writes to Karl in another letter, dated 10 February 1838:

"I will not lie to you and admit, that I am reproachful of myself for allowing you too much free reign. We

*have now reached the fourth month of the fiscal year
and you have already spent 280 thalers. This is more
than I have earned in the past winter... I am tired dear
Karl and will have to close shop."*

Heinrich Marx in fact did not only close his shop, but
also resigned from life and still died in the same year.
Father Heinrich Marx was clearly anxious of his son
squandering his inheritance and therefore dictated in
his testament, that an administrator would manage the
funds. He would have to regulate the manner in which
and when Karl Marx would be allowed to receive and
spend his inheritance. Under these circumstances it is
best we allow the poor soul, to give an own account of
his precarious situation. He thus wrote to an
acquaintance on the 25th January 1843:

*"As mentioned to you in my previous letters, my
familiar relationship has degenerated to an extent,
where I have no right to decree over my fortune as
long as my mother lives."*

This explains, why Marx was constantly strapped for
cash.

His friend Friedrich Engels, the son of a manufacturer
in Wuppertal, had no such problems. Similar to Marx,
he started writing political essays from an early age
and through regular exchanges with his friend had
compiled a small map of areas, where ignorance and
prejudice against foreign nations and their short-
comings were experienced. As typical example let us
listen to Engel's opinion of the Swiss in the year 1847:

"They are an incredibly snobbish nation of antediluvian sheepherders of the Alps, obstinate farmers and dirty bourgeois individuals, poor, but well-mannered, stupid, but devoted and committed to God, brutal, with wide-built shoulders, a small brain, but strong calves! Europe is left with only two areas, where wayward Christian-Germanic barbarism has remained untouched in its original form, almost to the point where they feed on acorns. These are Norway and the high Alps, i.e. original Switzerland. However, it now seems as though these moral conventions are due to be stirred from bottom up. The Execution-forces (German inter-state army) will hopefully do their utmost to meet their moral righteousness, elementary power and simple-mindedness with the appropriate force to principally destroy the same. But that will cause you Bourgeoisie to start whining! No poor, but satisfied shepherds, who seem to be so untroubled and uncaring, will be left to please you on your Sunday afternoon."

On 22 July 1853 Marx put his opinion about India down on paper:

"Indian society has absolutely no history, at least non that is known. What we acknowledge as history is none other than a sequence of events, whereby consecutive invaders have built their empires, based on the passive resistance of a society, which has remained true to its underlying principle of no resistance and has never changed."

Let us change the subject from Indians to Moors. On the 15th September 1857 Engels wrote an essay about "Algeria":

"Of all the inhabitants of Algeria, Moors are likely to be the least respected. They live in the urban areas and enjoy a higher living standard than the Arabs. As a result of their constant oppression by the Turkish rulers of the past, they are fearful, yet they have not lost their cruel ferociousness and vengefulness, and they have a very low standard in terms of moral righteousness."

Engels even went one step further in his letter to Marx on the 2nd November 1864. This time it was the Danish:

"I recently studied Friesian-Scandinavian philology and archaeology and have arrived at the conclusion, that the Danish are a pure nation of advocates, who are prepared to knowingly and unknowingly lie about academic or scientific questions in the interest of their party-political ideologies."

Neither were the French left unscathed by Engels. In 1841 he wrote:

"The French are obsessed by the idea that the river Rheine should be their property. The only dignified answer by the German nation to this presumptuous demand should be: 'Hand over Alsace-Lorraine!' Because I am of the opinion that the recapture of the German-speaking western banks of the Rheine is a

matter of national honour, while the Germanification of the renegade states Holland and Belgium has become a political necessity for us. Should we allow those countries to entirely oppress German nationhood, while the Slavic nations rise to become ever more powerful in the East?"

In 1854 Karl Marx spent some time studying the Islam. His appraisal did not result in a particularly squeamish verdict either:

"The Koran and its Muslim-based legislation reduce geography and ethnography of the various nations to an easy and convenient division into believers and non-believers. Non-believers are the so-called 'harby', in other words the enemy. Islam rejects nations which it regards as non-believers and thereby creates a situation of permanent enmity between the Muslims and the non-believers. Based on that concept, the ships of the buccaneers coming from the Berber states inherently played the role of the venerable fleet of the Islam."

Let us however sweep in front of our own doors and concentrate on Germany, of which Engels wrote benevolently in 1859:

"Germans have proven themselves as equals to other nations on all scientific levels for some time already and in most instances have proven their superiority to other civilized nations."

While being back in Germany let us have a quick and intimate look at the Marx-family, of which Karl did not have a particularly high opinion - neither of his own nor of the family of his friend Engels.

Thus Marx wrote to Engels in November 1848:

"Your old man is a swine to whom we will address a harshly worded letter."

Engels was employed as factory manager at his father's business branch situated in England. His father was a big capitalist from Wuppertal, who kept Engels on a financially tight leash, thereby preventing him from being able to meet all of Marx's financial wishes.

This caused Marx to write the following to Engels on the 29th November 1848:

"I have devised a reliable plan, how we can extort money from your old man, as we currently have none."

Engels neither seemed to be impressed with his father nor with the family business in Wuppertal. Permanent employment did not seem to be his forte either. Having only spent 14 days as employee of his father's factory, he wrote to Marx on 20 January 1845:

"This haggling is simply abominable, Wuppertal is abominable, this waste of time is abominable and especially abominable is the fact that I am not only Bourgeois, but have to take action against the proletariat as manufacturer and thus remain a

Bourgeoisie. Only a few days spent in the factory of my old man have made me aware again of this Abomination, which seems to have been lost to my memory previously. I obviously reckoned that I would remain in this hellhole as long as it would suit me with the idea that I would write something illegal, which would allow me to skip the border in a respectable manner. But it would seem as though I will not be able to push through until then. It is enough, I am leaving here come Easter."

Another Easter is approaching six years later and Engels has adjusted perfectly to his family- and work-surroundings and feels right at home:

"In view of me having been totally successful in subjecting my old man to an intrigue - at least until now - I am now able to settle in nicely. I will tell you of developments regarding my old man in person, as well as all of the intrigues, which I have spun around him, in order to prove my indispensability here on the one hand and to protect myself from being over-engaged in the trading house on the other hand. In another 6 weeks it is Easter anyway and it is an intricate matter. One thing is for sure, my old man will have to pay me in cash, especially once he has been here and I have properly buried him."

Marx spent a long time hoping for the day one of his uncles would die, thus writing to Engels on the 27th February 1852:

"The only good tidings which we have received from my sister in law, is the news that the indestructible uncle of my wife has fallen ill. Should the dog die now, I would be out of the woods."

Engels in turn held his thumbs for Marx, hoping that the uncle would die soon:

"As regards the news of the illness, which has befallen your uncle in Braunschweig, who stands in the way of you taking possession of your inheritance, I would like to congratulate and express my hope, that the catastrophe may run its course soon."

When the uncle finally passed away, Marx was so overjoyed, that he had to write another letter to Engels on the 8th of March 1855:

"Yesterday we received the news of 'a very happy event indeed', which is the announcement of the death of my wife's 90 years old uncle. My mother in law will therefore be able to save an annual annuity of 200 thalers and my wife will receive around 100 Pounds Sterling; possibly more if the dog has not included his housekeeper in his final will."

Karl Marx's mother did not exactly have an easy plight with her son. In a letter to Engels, Marx tells him on 31 March 1851:

"Then I wrote to my mother and threatened her that I would issue promissory notes against her name and if

she refuses to pay, I would return to Prussia and give myself up to the authorities!"

Marx experienced financial problems as long as he lived and was always ecstatic, when his attempt to borrow money, ended in success. On the 7th of May 1861 he was able to report a success to his friend Engels for a change:

"I have been able to extort 160 Pounds from my uncle, which allowed us to redeem the greater part of our liabilities. My mother, who hardly has any access to cash funds and is fast approaching her liquidation, destroyed a couple of promissory notes, which I previously issued in her favour."

On 6th November 1861, when Marx had been overtaken by his financial plights again, he wrote to Engels:

"I received an answer from my old lady yesterday. No more than 'loving' talk, but no cash. She then tells me what I already know, that she is 75 years of age and starts feeling some of the afflictions coming with age."

By the way, the favourite object of the two friends' blasphemy was Ferdinand Lassalle, who launched the workers union "Allgemeiner Deutscher Arbeiterverein" on the 23rd May 1863, out of which the political party "SPD" (Social Democratic Party of Germany) was borne later. He was not well-liked by Marx and Engels on account of his greater success and acceptance among German workers; it made them envious and hateful. Lassalle was borne in Breslau in 1825 and died in Geneva in 1864 in Geneva. He was a politician and writer. Lasalle, who came from a Jewish background, studied history and philosophy in Breslau and Berlin in the years 1842 to 1846. He was in favour- and supported the idea of holding general elections. But contrary to Karl Marx's conviction, Ferdinand Lassalle supported a kingdom founded on socialistic and democratic principles. Ferdinand Lassalle represented the countess Sophie Josepha von Hatzfeld, who was also his mistress, in a divorce suit lasting almost ten years and stayed in the countess' statehouse in Düsseldorf during the years 1850/51. Lassalle died at the age of 39 as a result of a serious shooting injury inflicted to his testis, following the challenge to a duel by the husband of his mistress.

Marx could not stand Lassalle. And so he wrote a letter to his good friend Engels on 30 July 1862:

"The Jewish nigger Lassalle, who fortunately leaves here at the end of the week, was fortunate to again lose 5 000 thalers through speculation. This oaf would rather recklessly lose money than he would loan it to a 'friend', who would guarantee him interest and capital. In the process he follows his belief that he needs to live the life of a Jewish baron or a baronized Jew. As said before, under different circumstances (and if he did not disturb my work), I would have found this oaf very amusing. Add to this his gorging eating habits and lewd rut of a so-called 'idealist'. Considering his education and hair growth on his head, I have arrived at the conclusion, that he is a descendant from the

blackamoors, who joined Moses' Exodus from Egypt (if his mother or grandmother from his father's side have not crossbred with a nigger). Well, the joining of Jewish and German lines with a basic substance of Negros is likely to result in a peculiar product. The intrusiveness of this fellow is very Nigger-like."

Interestingly enough, Marx himself was called "Mohr" (Moor) by his family and his friend Engels on account of his dark, frizzy mane. When considering his blasphemy against Jews, it should not be forgotten: Both grandfathers of Marx were rabbis!

Even though Marx and Engels were happy to regularly bad-mouth Lassalle, this did not keep Marx from accepting assistance from Lassalle, when it came to sourcing financial assistance from relatives.

Marx wrote to Lasalle on 15 February 1861:

"As you know, I would like to settle a couple of challenging financial matters with my uncle, who is managing my mother's fortune and has in the past granted me a number of substantial advances against that portion of the inheritance which becomes accruable to me in future. The man is ham-fisted, but he is a big fan of my writing. In your letter to me, you should therefore mention the tremendous success of my last piece (even though this does not apply) and need to make mention of our future plans of establishing a newspaper and such like."

Before that, Engels had written to Marx on the 7th of March 1856:

"As a typical Jew from the Slavic border area, Lassalle has always - under the guise of party politics - been ready to pounce on- and abuse everybody in his personal favour. Even worse and since long despicable is his obsession with becoming part of the high society, even if it is only for show, and in the process trying to hide the slimy Jew from Breslau under a thick coat of pomade and make-up."

Both really had not the least good to say about Lassalle. Marx wrote to Engels on 9 February 1860:

"Attached you will find the most recent letter from the kike Lassalle; you should keep it as a rarity. Imagine the plasticity of this least Greek-like water-Pollack of a Jew (Man denke sich die Plastizität dieses un-griechischsten aller wasserpolackischen Juden)."

As mentioned previously, Ferdinand Lasalle succumbed to his injuries resulting from a duel in Geneva on 31 August 1864. Obviously Marx and Engels could not let that incident pass without comment.

Engels wrote to Marx on 4 September 1864:

"Indescribable jubilation will have erupted amongst factory owners and the swine pushing for progress in view of the fact that Lassalle was probably the only chap in Germany itself, whom they feared. Quite

unbelievable is the manner in which he lost his life: To seriously fall in love with the daughter of a Bavarian envoy - this wannabee Don Juan - wanting to marry her, to be confronted by the shunned rival, who in any event is a gutless hustler, and to allow him to shoot you to death. That could only happen to Lassalle with his quaint mix of frivolity and sentimentality, Jewishness and wannabee-chivalry, which were so typical of him."

Engels further wrote to Marx about Lasalle's death on the 7th of November 1864:

"Lassalle seems to have succumbed to the fact, that he did not simply throw that human (referring to the lady, who was subject of the duel) on a bed in the boarding house and properly ravage her. She did not want his beautiful mind - she wanted his Jewish cock. It is the type of story that could only happen to Lassalle."

The countries, which later based their existence on the theories of Marx and Engels, typically thought of themselves as "worker and peasant states". Are they sure they understood the opinion of the two as regards peasants?

In 1845 Engels wrote an essay titled "Deutsche Zustände" (German affairs):

"The freedom-war against Napoleon of the years 1813/14 and 1815, the 'most glorious period of German history', as it is often described, was pure madness, which is more than likely to cause a number of honest and intelligent Germans to blush in future.

Sure, a considerable measure of enthusiasm could be witnessed at the time, but who were these enthusiasts? First and foremost these were peasants, the most stupid type of human on earth, a class, which supports feudalistic prejudice, rising in masses and similar to their fathers and those before them, prepared to rather die for those whom they called their Lords, than serve notice and discontinue their allegiance to a system, which boils down to being kicked and being beaten with horsewhips."

Engels gave peasants a tongue-lashing and Marx wrote down his opinion about peasants in 1853:

"Never in my life did I express an opinion, drunk or sober, that workers are just suited as cannon fodder, even though these lowlifes ('Knoten') ... barely regard them as being suitable as just that."

At the time the German expression "Knoten" was a derogatory term for young craftsmen and workers.

Marx wrote to an acquaintance in 1852:

"It seems unlikely that you will find more accomplished asses than these workers."

Of all people these two men, who served as anchor to all communist parties (thus the largest parties on earth), were men, who had a total dislike for parties!

Thus Engels wrote to Marx on 13 February 1851:

*"How do people such as us fit into a 'party',
considering that we avoid official appointments like the
pest? Of what use are we, who spit on the concept of
popularity and despise ourselves when we become
popular, to a 'party', in other words to a load of
donkeys, who rely on us, because they deem themselves
our equals? Truly, it will be no loss, if we are no
longer regarded as representatives of this pack of
dogs, which the past years' happenstance seems to
have brought on us."*

Both, Marx and Engels, got irritated with their
supporters time and again. In fact they apparently
sometimes regarded their theories to be misunderstood.
They saw, that people were starting to call themselves
"Marxists". However it seems as though Marx and
Engels had a hard time to align themselves with these
self-proclaimed "Marxists". This caused Marx to write
down the legendary sentence:

"All I know is that I am not a Marxist."

Of all people, the Russians, who as from 1917 became
the biggest fans of Marx and Engels, came off
particularly badly.

In 1855 Engels wrote:

*"Russians of all classes to this day remain much too
barbaric to find pleasure in taking part in any form of
scientific or intellectual activities, with the exception of
intrigues. For that reason you will find that most of the
exceptional persons in their military service are*

foreigners or for that matter 'Ostseiskije', which are Germans from their Baltic states."

Pan-Slavism was a movement in the 19th century, which aimed at uniting all Slavs into a single empire. Neither Marx nor Engels had much time for this movement. As an example you might consider an essay, which Engels wrote in 1855 titled "Germany and Pan-Slavism" (Deutschland und der Panslawismus):

"Pan-Slavism is the result of a mind change from a confession of faith to a political programme, which has 800 000 bayonets at its disposal. It leaves Europe with only one alternative: Subjugation under the Slavs or the permanent destruction of their offensive centre - Russia."

In 1846 the United States declared war on Mexico. The war was ended in 1848 with the USA ending up as the winner. Most interestingly Marx and Engels turned out to be fans of the US-army.

In the "Neue Rheinische Zeitung", a newspaper, which was brought out by the two friends, Engels published the following article on the 15th of February 1849:

"Should it be regarded as bad luck that the beautiful and splendid state of California has been taken from the lazy Mexicans, who in any event did not know what to do with it? Should it be regarded as bad luck if the energetic Yankees substantially increase currency on account of their quick exploitation of the gold mines

found in this place, ideally located at a point adjacent to the quite Pacific Ocean, where they will in just a few years concentrate a dense population and an extensive trade, create big cities and steamer links to the world, construct railway lines from New York to San Francisco, open up the Pacific for civilisation, and for the third time in history are likely to steer the world's trade into a new direction? The 'independence' of a few Hispanic Californians and Texans might be adversely affected by this development, while 'justice' and similar principles might have been negatively affected here and there; but of what importance are these minor infringements if weighed against the bigger picture of the world's history?"

Marx and Engels also spent time considering the readers of their books. Marx wrote to Engels on 15 August 1857:

"It is quite possible that I make a fool of myself. Such incidents can best be parried by making use of dialectics. I have always compiled my assertions such, that I will be proven to be correct, even if the inverse assumption is made."

Engels urged Marx on in a letter dated 31 January 1860:

"Start being less conscientious in all of your own affairs; it (referring to the book 'Das Kapital') still remains far too good for the lousy public. That this thing is being written and published is of main importance; all of the weaknesses which are

conspicuous to your eye, will never be identified by the ignorant asses out there."

Marx, whose family converted from the Jewish confession to that of Protestants, regularly committed acts of blasphemy against the Jewish faith. In that regard he wrote an essay titled "The question of the Jews" (Zur Judenfrage) in 1848:

"Let us have a look at the true worldly Jew, not the Jew honouring the Sabbath, but the average everyday Jew. Let us search for the mystery of the religion within the true Jew instead of the mystery of the Jew within his faith. What is the worldly reason for the existence of Judaism? It is the practical existence of needs, self-interest. What is the worldly cult of the Jew? Being a haggler. Which is his true god? Money. So be it! Thus the self-emancipation of our time may be likened to the emancipation of a haggler and money, in other words of practical and real Judaism. In the Jewish faith we can therefore recognize a general and ever-present antisocial element, which in its historic development - to which the Jews to their disgrace have assiduously contributed - has reached a new height. A height which needs to be destroyed and dissolved. The Jewish emancipation in its current form and standing is the emancipation of mankind emerging from Judaism."

On 13 March 1843 made more unsavoury remarks about the Jewish faith in a letter to an acquaintance:

"A moment ago the leader of the local Israelites came to me with the request to prepare and submit a petition to parliament on behalf of the Jews - and I will do it. As repulsive as I find the Israelite faith, ... it is incumbent on us to open up as many as possible fronts in our advance against the Christian state and secretly introduce sensible matters."

Engels was much the same, writing in the "Neue Rheinische Zeitung" on 29 April 1849:

"Readers of the 'Neue Rheinische Zeitung' will recall, that the national dimwits and money grubbers of the quagmire in Frankfurt, which is regarded as a parliament, have always counted the polish Jews as being part of the Germans, although this smuttiest of all nations cannot be seen to be related to Frankfurters - neither based on their jargon nor by descent - except possibly for their worthiness as regards profits."

Engels was no particular friend of Europe's small nations. In this regard he wrote in the "Neue Rheinische Zeitung" on 13 January 1849:

"Among all of the nations and smaller nationalities which form part of Austria you will find only three, which actively shaped history and brought progress, thereby remaining viable - the German, the Polish, the Hungarians. That is the reason for them now being revolutionaries. All of the other bigger and smaller tribes have a duty to disintegrate as part of the worldwide revolutionary storm. That is the reason, why they are now contra-revolutionary. Try to find one

among these tribes, Czechs and Serbs included, which can present a history of national traditions, which is inherent to this nation and stands out above the smaller local conflicts?

In Europe no country can be found, that does not have a hidden corner somewhere, hiding one or more of the ruins of tribes and nations, which are leftovers of residents, which have been pushed back and subjugated by the larger nation, which later became the mainstay of the country's historic development. The remainders of nations, which have been mercilessly crushed by the greater, as Hegel would have it. This remaining waste of nations always is and will remain fanatical supporters of the contra-revolution until they have been fully eradicated or denationalized. Already their mere existence is by nature a protest against the big historic revolution. Thus the Gaelic are found in Scotland, the supporters of the Stuarts from 1640 to 1745. Similarly the Bretons of France, who supported the Bourbons from 1792 to 1800. And so we have the Basks of Spain, supporters of Don Carlos. In Austria you will find the pan-Slavic southern Slavs, which are no more than the waste of a nation resulting from a very confused history reaching back a thousand years."

Austria-Hungary was a favourite topic of these two philosophers. Apart from people of German descent and Hungarians this great empire also comprised of many Slavic nationalities. Neither Marx nor Engels could stand these nations and emphasised this time and again.

Thus Marx wrote in the "Neue Rheinische Zeitung" on the 1st of January 1849:

"The defeat of the workers' class in France and thus the victory of the French bourgeoisie were simultaneously the victory of east over west and thus the defeat of civilisation by barbarians. The suppression of the Romans by the Russians and their instrument - the Turks -, started in Wallachia. Croats, Hussars, Czechs, Sereczyns and similar rogues strangled the Germanic freedom in Vienna, and in this very moment the Tsar is omnipresent in Europe."

On the 13th of January 1849 Engels wrote in the "Neue Rheinische Zeitung":

"As soon as the French proletariat stage their first victorious uprising, which the French emperor seems to deliberately provoke, the Austrian Germans and Hungarians will be free and they will take bloody revenge on the Slavic barbarians. The big war, which will inevitably result, will destroy this special Slavic bond and will remove all of these small stubborn nations from history except for their names. The next world war will not only remove reactionary classes and dynasties, but will entirely remove reactionary nations from this world. And that too will be a form of progress."

A mere month later the following text of Engels was published in the "Neue Rheinische Zeitung":

"We repeat: Except for the Polish, the Russians and possibly the Slavs of Turkey, no Slavic nation has a future, for the simple reason, that all of the remaining Slavs lack the fundamental precondition of historic, geographic, political and industrial independence and viability. The Czechs have no history, and in this instance we include the Moravians and Slovak, even though their language and history differ. Bohemia has been attached to Germany since the time of Carl, the Great. For a moment you found the Czech nation emancipating and thus establishing the Great Moravian Empire, only to after a short while find them being enslaved once again and become a pawn, which is passed to- and fro between Germany, Hungary and Poland. Finally Bohemia and Monrovia become a definite part of Germany and all other Slavic regions remain aligned to Hungary. And now this historically non-existent 'nation' demand independence? The same applies to the southern Slavs. Germany and Hungary are denied access to the Adriatic Sea by the Slovenes and Croats; and for geographic and commercial reasons Germany and Hungary cannot allow themselves to be cut off from the Adriatic Sea, this being of greatest importance to their continued existence and survival, similar to the example, whereby Poland needs access to the coast of the Baltic Sea stretching from Gdansk to Riga. For sure such requirements cannot be turned into reality without making use of force in order to bend one or the other young and budding nation. Because without applying force and in the absence of a historic ruthlessness nothing could have been achieved in history, and if Alexander, Caesar or Napoleon would have been

*doomed to remain as immobilized as the potential
immobility, which the pan-Slavs appeal for on behalf of
their degenerate customers, what would have been the
impact on history? And surely the Persians, Celts and
Christian Germans should be advanced in favour of
the Czechs, Ogulians and Sereczyns?"*

In 1853 Marx wrote about the same subject:

*"The Germans and Scandinavians, which both belong
to the same great race, will only prepare the road for
their archenemy - the Slavs - if they fight with each
other instead of forming a union."*

Engels was of the opinion that the Slavs were ungrateful. The Germans and Hungarians had after all brought
them civilisation. It would seem as though the 15th of
February 1849 was a very busy day for him, as he published much news in the "Neue Rheinische Zeitung":

*"The independent Bohemian-Moravian state is wedged
in-between Silesia and Austria, with Austria and Styria
being denied its natural access to the Adriatic Sea and
the Mediterranean Sea by the 'Republic of southern
Slavs', while Germany's tattered eastern regions seem
like a piece of bread having been nibbled on by rats!
And all of this is the result of the obstinate Czechs and
Slav showing their appreciation to the Germans, who
have made the effort of bringing them civilisation,
agriculture and education! Which then are the
supposedly great and terrible acts of wrongdoing,
which the Germans have carried out against the Slavic
nation? The Germans recaptured the previously*

German and later Slavic part of the north, which stretches from the river Elbe right back to the Warthe-river; a conquest, which was necessitated by 'geographical and strategic needs', which resulted from the break-up of the Carolingian empire. That this conquest was made in the interest of civilisation has not been disputed to this day. To make a long story short, it has become evident, that these so-called 'crimes' committed by Germans and Hungarians against the questionable Slavs should be regarded as some of the greatest and commendable deeds, which are attributable to our and the Hungarian Nations."

In the same edition of the "Neue Rheinische Zeitung" of 15 February 1849, Engels even glorifies the hatred of Slavic Russians as a revolutionary act:

"In answer to the sentimental utterings made in support of a brotherhood, as presented to us on behalf of the contra-revolutionary nations of Europe, we reply that the hate of Russians always was - and remains - the first revolutionary passion of the German nation, and that an additional hatred for the Czechs and Croats has developed after the start of the revolution and that we, jointly with the Polish and the Hungarians, will only be able to secure the revolution by resorting to a decisive measure of terror against these Slavic nations. What follows, is war, an unforgiving battle for live and death against the Slavs betraying the revolution; a battle of annihilation and ruthless terror - not in the interest of Germany, but the interest of the revolution!"

One day later Engels goes one step further. In the edition of 16 February 1849 he makes it clear that he regards the Slavs as being blockheads, who are stupid enough to actually contribute towards their own oppression:

"Any other nation would have harboured an uncontained hatred for an oppressor who has just bombarded a city such as Prague. But what did the Czechs do? They kissed the whip, which has just flogged them down to the flesh, they vowed faith to the flag, under which their brethren were massacred and their women were raped. The street fights of Prague essentially are the turning-point for the Austrian democratic pan-Slavs. Recognizing the prospect of obtaining their miserable 'national independence' they sold out democracy, in effect they sold the revolution to the all-encompassing Austrian monarchy. And for this cowardly, vile betrayal of the revolution we will one day exact bloody revenge on the Slavs."

In 1852 Karl Marx received mail in London from Müller-Tellering, a former colleague of his at the "Neue Rheinische Zeitung". In a letter to another acquaintance on 10 May 1852, Marx expresses his agitation about his ex-colleague:

"Attached you will find a postal envelope, which the useless and half-crazy coward, Müller-Tellering, mailed to me. Address: Charles Marx, the future dictator of Germany." (It's original wording in in the English language)

On 23 May 1851 it was Engels who in turn wrote a letter to Marx expressing his hostility towards the Polish:

"The more I think about history, the more I come to realize, that the Polish are essentially a nation which has outlived its usefulness, the more I understand that they should simply be used as means for the time being, until Russia itself has been pulled into- and joins the agrarian revolution. When that moment dawns, Poland has no further right to exist. During history the Polish have never done anything but committing towards stupid acts, based on courage and a love for brawls. Not even a single moment can be named, when the Polish were able to do anything which contributed towards progress or did something which was of historic significance."

On 22 September 1854 Marx wrote to Engels discussing an acquaintance:

"Püttmann, that fat pig, has have been sent from here to Australia as a 'colonialist' along with his family."

And in 1854 Marx is convinced once again that he has discovered evil Jews:

"The growing dependence of the Kaiser on the Jews of the Bank in Vienna remains in step with the increasing military character of his reign."

On 14 April 1856 Engels writes another letter to Marx, in which he again slanders Lassalle's name:

"I have been much amused by the Lassallians again. The ruffled Jew-head must be quite a sight, settled on top of his red pyjama-coat and the draping of the marquise-bed, with his polack-ish pride becoming visible each time he moves. This oaf must leave a very lousy-repulsive impression."

On 17 December 1858 it was the turn of the citizens of Baden (Germany) to be at the receiving end, when Marx wrote to Engels:

"The pathetic bustle of these small Badensic fleas, which have been bred out by the democratic cesspool is touching."

On 22 September 1859 Engels tells his friend Marx of a misfortune:

"Just a few days before my old man arrived, I had some very damned luck. Having joined a few people in the local pub, an unknown Englishman insulted me and with me holding my umbrella, I hit him and the tip hit him in the eye."

Wilhelm Liebknecht (1826-1900) was one of the most renowned founders of the political party SPD. He becomes the subject matter of a letter by Marx to Engels on the 25th May 1859:

"Liebknecht is of no use as author apart from being unreliable and weak of character, which I will write more about in due course. This oaf would most certainly have been on the receiving end of a kick in

the butt this week, signalling his departure, if it had not been for certain circumstances, which force us to keep him on as a scare crow for the time being."

Wilhelm Liebknecht would still become the target for further slander by these two. But before this, Marx wrote to Engels on the 6th of February 1865, telling him about an article of his, which had been published in the magazine "Social-Demokrat":

"It is fortunate, that in the newest 'Social-Demokrat' which arrived today, your appeal to slay the aristocrats, has been published right after my article."

Engels did not have a particularly high opinion of the editors of the "Social-Demokrat" and wrote to Marx on 1 December 1865:

"It is quite telling of their riffraff-character that the gentlemen from the 'Social-Demokrat' are trying to reconnect with us. They seem to regard everybody to be similar shitheads as they are."

Marx remarked to Engels on 10 February 1866:

"I am going to read this Wilhelm Liebknecht the riot act as regards his faintheartedness. It is after all our aim to witness the demise of the 'Social-Demokrat' and this whole Lassalle-shit."

Marx to Engels on 10 August 1869:

"You will find the printed part of Wilhelm Liebknecht's oration in the attachment ... behind his inherent stupidity hides an undeniable measure of astuteness, whereby he crafts the content to fit his agenda ... This brute believes in a future 'Democratic State'! Unchecked, this will essentially be the same as a constitutionalized England, before you know a commoner-orientated United States or even a miserable Switzerland. 'It' absolutely has no idea what revolutionary politics comprise of."

Marx to Engels on 12 February 1870:

"A very nicely executed double-punch against Wilhelm Liebknecht of the populist party, as well as against this Swiss and his band of rascals! As regards the apology of Wilhelm Liebknecht, one never knows whether he is lying deliberately or whether a thousand thoughts are milling around in his confused head."

Similarly agitated, it was Engels, who wrote about the journalist Heinrich Beta in a letter to Marx on the 11th of December 1859:

"Beta is the biggest swine I have ever encountered. That trashy article of his has me enraged me hugely. Unfortunately this oaf is such a cripple, that one can hardly beat him any further; let it be said that this mongrel needs to face our personal wrath one day."

Marx was often financially supported by the poet Ferdinand Freiligrath. When he could no longer afford this assistance, Marx wrote to Engels about the poet on 7 June 1859:

"As regards Freiligrath. Between you and me, he is a shithead."

When Freiligrath refused to testify in favour of Marx in a court matter, Marx resorted to threatening him with the possibility of reporting him to the Prussian police and denunciating him. On 23 February 1860 wrote directly to Freiligrath:

"You are aware of the fact that I have in my possession at least 200 letters, which you sent me, containing - if need be - more than enough information to suggest an existing association between you and me, as well as the communist party."

Marx could never resist slandering the Jews and thus he wrote about a certain Mr Levy of London in his book titled "Herr Vogt" in November 1860:

"While the newspaper 'Weekly Mail' insists that Levy does not pretend that an X should be understood to be a U (a common German figure of speech similar to this English one: 'Leading you up the garden path'), he certainly seems to pretend that a Y should be understood to be an I. In fact you will not find a single Levi spelt with a Y amongst the 22 000 Levis, which Moses counted as part of his people when he lead them through the desert to the Promised Land. Similar to Edouard Simon, who with all of his might would like to be part of the Roman race, Levy would like to belong to

the race of the Anglo-Saxons. For that reason he makes a point of criticizing the anti-English politics of a Mr Disraeli at least once a month, as Disraeli, 'this Asian mystery', does not originate from the Anglo-Saxon race. But of what use is it for Levy to attack Mr Disraeli and pretend that a Y has become an I, when mother nature has clearly inscribed his bloodline most peculiarly in Gothic lettering, right in the middle of his face."

On 24 March 1861 Marx wrote to his niece Antoinette Philips:

"This young lady (Fräulein), who literally threatened to drown me in kind goodwill, must be the most ugly being that I have come across in my whole life, featuring a nasty Jewish physiognomy."

On 18 June 1862 Marx shared his distress with his financier Engels:

"I find it revolting to keep you busy once again with my personal misfortune, but what can I do? No day goes past without my wife telling me that she wished that she would lie in her grave with her children alongside her, and when I consider the humiliation, torment and fear which they have to experience under the current situation, I have to admit, that truly cannot blame her. As you would know, I have spent the 50 Pounds on redeeming previous debts. From personal experience you would know though, that there will always be current expenditure that needs to be paid in cash. We were able to do so by once again pawning off

the goods, which we were only able to recover from the pawn shop at the end of April. But on account of this source having run dry for a number of weeks now, my wife unsuccessfully resorted to flogging some of my books a week ago. I feel so sorry for the children.

I make a point of extending the texts of the current book as it would seem as though the German dogs assess the value of a book according to its cubic content.

I receive no visitors and I prefer it that way, as the type of mankind found here, is welcome to come kiss me ---. Fine vermin!"

In order to lay his hands on money, Engels gives the following advice to Marx on 8 August 1862:

"Unless we discover the art of shitting gold, you will probably have no other choice, but to find ways and means, how you can extort money from your relatives."

The long-time partner and common law spouse of Engels, Mary, died in 1863. In this regard Marx wrote to him on the 8th of January 1863:

"The tiding of the passing of your friend Mary has saddened me just as much as it has upset you. She was sweet-natured, funny and was very attached to you. Why in the devil's name has so much bad luck occurred in our midst? Things are becoming too much and I do not know where to next. I am unable to freely express my opinion to any person in the whole of London, and at home I simply play the role of the quiet stoic in order to counter the outbursts from the other

side. Work under such circumstances becomes impossible. Instead of Mary, could it not have been my mother, who has fully lived her life and is straddled with physical inabilities...?
As you can see, the thoughts entering the mind of the 'civilised' are quite remarkable under certain circumstances. Greetings, your K.M.
NB: How will you set up your establishment in future? It is an extraordinary challenge for you, considering that in finding Mary you also found a home for yourself, free and withdrawn from the scum of this earth, whenever you chose to be so."

Engels felt extremely offended by the rather superficial commiserations of his friend and wrote to Marx on 13 January 1863:

"I trust you find it in order, if I only answered you belatedly considering your frosty attitude in addressing my personal misfortunes, which I found hard to bear. Under the circumstances of this loss, which was always likely to be hard on me, all of my friends, including Philistine acquaintances, have shown me more sympathy and friendship than I could ever have expected. You found this to be the ideal moment to prove your superior mentality in calmly analysing this incident from a distance."

But both made up again after Marx offered his apology. And thus Marx wrote to Engels on the 12th September 1863:

"The most interesting acquaintance I have made here is that of a certain Colonel Lapinski. He is in any case the most ingenious Pole - a man of action - I have gotten to know. Instead of a conflict among nations all he knows is the fight against races. He hates all people from the orient, among which he indiscriminately counts Russians, Turks, Greeks, Armenians, etc. His purpose for being in London now, is that of mustering a German legion of at least 200 men, with which he will confront the Russians in Poland under the black-red-golden flag."

In 1867 Marx wrote in his famous book "Das Kapital":

"A capitalist understands well, that all goods, no matter how shabby they appear to be or badly they smell, are by virtue of believing them to be- as well as in fact represent money - thus inherently representing circumcised Jews - while they are miraculous means, allowing more money to be made of money."

Though, after colleagues, relatives and ethnic groups had been the subject of Marx' and Engels' slander, they now strike out at a totally different type of person.

Engels wrote to Marx from Manchester on 21 July 1868:

"Who is this pansy Dr Boruttau, who appears to be rather highly-strung as regards love among same sex?"

Marx answered Engels and wrote from London on the 23rd of July 1868:

"I do not know much about Dr Boruttau, the faggot, except that he is 'busy' among the Lassalleans (fraction of Schweitzer)."

The two gentlemen discussed here, are Carl Boruttau, a doctor and social democrat, and Johann Baptist von Schweitzer, who also was a social democrat, involved since the start of its early beginnings. In 1868 Schweitzer, the later to be Chairman of the General German Workers' Association (ADAV) was incarcerated on the charge of "unnatural fornication" with a bricklayer. The polemic publication of a judicial pamphlet by a certain Karl Heinrich Ulrichs in favour of Schweitzer ended in failure. Around this same time this man, Ulrichs sent his theoretical main edition of "Memnon" (Mammon), which aimed at having § 175 struck from the statutes while also lobbying for the social acceptance of homo-sexual relationships, to Karl Marx. In his compositions Ulrichs called homosexuals "Urninge", i.e. "Urninden". Marx passed the book onto Friedrich Engels, and Engels then wrote his friend Marx a letter on 22 June 1869:

"That is quite a curious 'Urning' which you have sent to me. These are some very unnatural revelations. The pederasts are clearly starting to find each other and are taking stock, so as to become a force within the state. Currently the only thing missing is a formal organisation, but it seems as though it is secretly inexistence already. Considering they can count on

reputable names such as Rösing and Schweitzer in the old and even in the new parties, their success will not have us waiting. 'War against the snatches, peace to the arseholes' will become our credo. We are lucky that personally we are too old, that we need to fear the victory of such a party and will be expected to pay physical tribute to the victors. But what of the young generation! And by the way, this is only possible in Germany, where such a fellow can turn a piggish mess into a theory and extends an invitation to all: introït, etc. Unfortunately he does not as yet have the courage, to publically out himself and openly admit himself to be an 'it' , and so he needs to continue coram publico to do it 'from the front', although he might not do it 'from the front into', as he inadvertently indicated once. But wait and see, once the new penal law of northern Germany has acknowledged the rights of the arse, then things are about to seriously change. We, the poor people, who have a child-like preference for women and take it from the front, will have a hard time. If Schweitzer could be of service, then that would have to be him making an effort in extracting the personal details of all of the high and highest-ranking pederasts from this quaint and strange personality. Considering their common congeniality, it should not be too much of a challenge."

Marx, similar to most of his contemporaries regarded Russia to be the epitome of backwardness and thus wrote to an acquaintance on 17 February 1870:

"The obvious fact that the Russian state represents the Mongolians as part of its political relationship and

negotiations with Europe and America has generally become part of common knowledge."

The German-French war broke out in 1870. In that regard Marx wrote to Engels on 20th July 1870:

"The French need a hiding. Should the Prussians be victorious, then the centralisation of political power will be of good use to the German workers' class. The German predominance will move the centre of gravity of the western European labour movement from France to Germany. One just needs to review the developments of the movement in both countries from 1866 until now, to understand that the German workers' class outperforms the French as regards theoretical and organisational capacities. Their predominance over the French within the greater picture of world politics would simultaneously represent the predominance of our theory over the Proudhons (Marx' and Engels' French counterpart)."

Pierre-Joseph Proudhon was an economist and theorizer of the concept of anarchy.

In a letter to his daughter Laura and his son in law, Paul Lafargue, Marx once again wrote about the German-French war on 28 July 1870:

"Personally I would be in favour of both, the Prussians and French, taking turns in striking out at each other, and that - as I have to assume - the German will ultimately be victorious. I wish this, because the

*definitive defeat of the French emperor is likely to
result in a French revolution."*

Even philosophers like to go on holiday once in a
while. Marx did not send a postcard, but wrote a little
trip report to Engels on the 14th of August 1879:

*"We were fortunate this morning, when we inquired at
the Hôtel de l'Europe, because as luck would have it,
60 French were in the preparing to depart, whereas the
steamships with their fresh load of human waste had
not yet arrived."*

On 25 August 1879 Marx wrote to Engels about an
English sea resort at Ramsgate:

"Many Jews and fleas to be found here."

But enough of the holiday experience. Let us go back
to the newspapers. On the 2nd of February 1881,
Engels revealed the secret of success of the "Neue
Rheinische Zeitung", which had been discontinued in
the meantime, to an acquaintance:

*"It was our disdain for- and the mockery of our
adversaries, which allowed us to secure 6 000
subscribers in just 6 months."*

In 1882 Marx was already marked by a serious medical
condition. On 11 November 1882 he wrote about his
two sons in laws to Engels from London:

"Lafargue has this serious scar of the negro-nation: no sense of shamefacedness when he runs the risk of becoming laughing stock. In actual fact Lafargue is the last scholar of Bakunin, who seriously believes in him. Longuet as last Proudhonist and Lafargue as the last Bakuninist! May they go to hell!"

Marx was already irritated with his future son in law Paul Lafargue, when he was still courting Marx' daughter Laura. Lafargue even remained in the house of Marx, when his fiancée Laura Marx had gone out. On 20th March 1866 an irritated Karl Marx wrote to Laura:

"This damned rascal Lafargue harasses me with his Proudhonism and apparently is not willing to stop, until I have properly bashed in his Creole-skull."

Paul Lafargue was ambitious and made himself available as candidate in the communal elections of Paris. He ended up as candidate of the local constituency Jardin des Plantes, which district was home to the Zoo of Paris. Lafargue was a French Creole who stemmed from African forefathers. On 26 April 1887 Engels wrote a letter to the wife of Paul Lafargues, the daughter of Karl Marx. In it he gave his commentary about the fact that Lafargue was the candidate for a district, in which Paris' Zoo was to be found:

"Being a Negro, Lafargue inherently stands much closer to the animal kingdom than the rest of us, which makes him the ideal representative of this district."

Even when he got older, Engels made no bones about his total dislike of the Slavs and so he wrote to an acquaintance on 7 February 1882:

"Now you may ask me, whether I have no sympathies for the smaller Slavic nations and their left-over tribes - in fact damned little."

Only two weeks later, on the 22nd February 1882, Engels wrote about the same issue to the same acquaintance:

"I am sufficiently authoritarian to regard the existence of such primitive folk in the middle of Europe as an anachronism. They and their right to cattle rustling have to be sacrificed without mercy in the interest of the European proletariat."

Remaining in contact with the leadership of the Lassalleans, Wilhelm Liebknecht in 1875 initiated the "Gothaen Programme". In his written critique Marx literally destroyed this programme. The authors of the "Gothaen programme" were able to keep this critical article away from the public eye for a very long time. In the beginning of the 1890's Engels successfully pushed through the publication of the "Critique of the Gothean Programme" (Kritik des Gothaer Programms) and in the process became the subject of clear displeasure and indignation by Liebknecht and others.

On 11th February Engels wrote to an acquaintance:

"Obviously Liebknecht is furious because the critique is mainly aimed at him, who is the father figure, who generated this despicable programme together with that bum-fucker Hasselmann."

By the way, the person called "bum-fucker" in this case is none other than Wilhem Hasselmann, who was one of the leaders of the previously mentioned ADAV, which had been founded by Lassalle.

Now that we have heard all of Marx' and Engels' sound bites, Engels writes something astonishing on the 19th of April 1890:

"Anti-Semitism is thus no more than the reaction of a dying social order dating back to the middle ages, which finds it difficult to come to terms with modern society, which mainly comprises of capitalists and wage earners, and therefore only serves the interests of reactionary forces under an apparent social cloak; it is a variation of feudal socialism, for which we should have no time. If it is practised in a country, it is a clear indication, that there is not enough capital. In these times capital and wage labour are inseparable. The stronger the capital, the stronger the class of wage earners, which in turn brings us closer to the demise of capital-rule. My wish for the Germans, which includes the Viennese, is that we experience a fast growth of capitalist development and not a slowdown with them disappearing in an abyss. The situation is worsened by the fact that anti-Semitism actually skews the situation. 'It' does not even recognize and understand the Jews, which it now tries to denunciate. Otherwise it would

know, that on account of the actions of east-European anti-Semitists, you find thousands upon thousands of Jewish proletarians here in England and in America, and the same applies to Turkey on account of the Spanish inquisition; and these Jewish workers belong to that part of the labour force, which has been abused most and live under the most squalid circumstances. Here in England we have experienced three strike actions by Jewish workers over the past twelve months and then we are expected to take active part in anti-Semitism as a so-called struggle against organised capital? Apart from that we owe the Jews too much. Ignoring Heine and Börne for a moment, then it needs to be remembered that Marx was a true-blooded Jew; Lassalle was a Jew. Many of our best people are Jews. My friend Victor Adler, who currently sits incarcerated in a jail in Vienna, finds himself atoning for his devotion for our cause. Eduard Bernstein, the editor of the 'London Sozialdemokrat', Paul Singer, one of our representatives in the German 'Reichstag', - these are all men which I proudly regard as my friends, and they are all Jews!"

Ladies and gentlemen, this brings us to the end of our presentation! Surely these two men also spoke and wrote of pleasant matters, but that would have been boring. Essentially we really do not care that much what you think of Marx and Engels. We were simply surprised to read these sound bites and utterings, making us wonder, whether other people would be just as astonished! The accuracy and integrity of these quotes can be tested quite easily, just have a look around you.

Just one moment! We still have one last snippet:

Did you know that the slogan "Workers of the world, unite!" was not conceived by Karl Marx?

That one he pinched from a man by the name of Karl Schapper.

Source:

"Marx-Engels-Werke", Archive of the Institute for Marxism-Leninism of the Central Committee of the SED-party (East-Berlin), "Marx-Engels-Gesamtausgabe", Archive of the Marx-Engels-Institute (Moscow) and other books and documents

Publisher:

Björn Akstinat

Author, publisher, media consultant, university lecturer and founder of the organisation "Internationale Medienhilfe" (IMH), which is active on a world-wide scale.

Simon Akstinat

Author of a number of non-fiction books, audio books and photo books.

www.ingramcontent.com/pod-product-compliance
Lightning Source LLC
LaVergne TN
LVHW021314200726
843509LV00012B/1917